M000087235

TENNESSEE
Simply Beautiful

PHOTOGRAPHY AND TEXT BY **BOB SCHATZ**

INTRODUCTION BY **TIPPER GORE**

TITLE PAGE: Flowering dogwood trees on the banks of the Little River. The river runs alongside Laurel Creek Road in the Great Smoky Mountains National Park.

RIGHT: Deciduous trees in Cades Cove, Great Smoky Mountains, flame with fall color.

FRONT COVER: The rusting roof of a barn is framed by the spring green of Water Valley. This view can easily be found at the Water Valley Overlook just off the Natchez Trace Parkway.

BACK COVER: The Tennessee state capitol, completed in 1859, is the second oldest state capitol still in use. The building's architect William Strickland, died during the construction and is buried just above the capitol's cornerstone. The capitol grounds are the final resting place for President James K. Polk.

FRONT FLAP: Union Station in downtown Nashville was the main departure point for middle-Tennessee soldiers of the two world wars. After rail service ceased in 1976, the station was converted into a magnificent hotel.

ISBN 1-56037-359-8
Photography © 2005 by Bob Schatz
© 2005 Farcountry Press
Text by Bob Schatz
Foreword by Tipper Gore

This book may not be reproduced in whole or in part by any means (with the exception of short quotes for the purpose of review) without the permission of the publisher.

For more information about our books write Farcountry Press, P.O. Box 5630, Helena, MT 59604; call (800) 821-3874; or visit www.farcountrypress.com.

Created, produced, and designed in the United States.
Printed in China.

09 08 07 06 05   1 2 3 4 5

At 256 feet in height, Fall Creek Falls is one of the tallest waterfalls east of the Rocky Mountains. Located near Spencer in Fall Creek Falls State Park, the waterfalls and pool below are a summertime favorites.

INTRODUCTION *by* TIPPER GORE

I am honored to contribute to this extraordinary book of photographs celebrating the natural beauty and diversity of the great state of Tennessee. In years of looking through his camera lens, Bob Schatz has captured the visual splendor of the state, from the breathtaking beauty of the Delta flatlands and the river city of Memphis—birthplace of the blues—to the timeless mystery of the Great Smoky Mountains in the east. He has focused on nature, architecture, history, and culture in his unique portrait of the diversity, raw beauty, and eternal spirit of our state.

Bob has been an artist his entire life. He remembers sneaking his father's camera out of the closet when he was four years old to try to discern its mysteries. He received a Brownie camera from his neighbor in the third grade and, by high school, Bob was taking photographs for the yearbook and newspaper. His passion for photography was confirmed when he discovered the magic of watching his images emerge in the darkroom.

It was a passion well worth pursuing. He has depicted, in this book, the lush greens of rolling hills in summer and the reds of the Cumberland Plateau in autumn. He presents photographs of industrial sites as well as historic buildings, such as the old tobacco barns in Smithville. Who can forget Lynchburg's very own Jack Daniels Distillery? As much as I have explored and traveled this varied state, what thrills me the most about Bob's work is seeing how hidden surprises in well-known places catch his eye: Jackson Falls on the Natchez Trace Parkway or Chucalissa, the prehistoric American Indian village dating back to A.D. 1000, near Memphis. These photographs awaken a fresh desire to see anew the natural wonders that he has portrayed in this remarkable book.

These photographs also bring back many memories for me. My family and I spent countless summers on Center Hill Lake, which is 20 minutes from our Carthage farm. Bob shows the serenity and enchantment of this amazing manmade lake, which is visited by so many middle-Tennesseans.

A January snow dusts ferns and a mossy log on the Sugarlands Trail in Great Smoky Mountains National Park.

When I see his photograph of Reelfoot Lake, I remember taking my children there to this special place where eagles nest amid the surreal cypress trees. Reelfoot Lake was created by an earthquake in 1912 that rang church bells as far away as Boston. Today it is one of the most important flyways in the country for migrating waterfowl. I always have the feeling that I have journeyed back in time when I am there.

Bob was an only child and enjoyed a close relationship with both of his parents. His mother was from Eagleville, Tennessee, and his father was from Birmingham, Alabama. It was his mother who trained his eye by drawing his attention to a beautiful sunset, flower, or tree. His mother was the person who focused him, Bob says, on "seeing the beauty that is all around us every day."

Bob's father—who was an academic dean at Belmont University in Nashville—commuted from the Eagleville home of Bob's great-grandmother, taking young Bob with him. It was his father who enticed his six-year-old son to rise early for the long drive, with the promise of seeing the sunrise at Radnor Lake in Nashville. These images remain close to his heart: the early morning dew, the fog on the lake, and the abundant wildlife in the area. Bob's love for the land was obviously born from these early experiences.

Bob learned from childhood that light can bring a photograph to life and give it nuance.

Actors dressed as Confederate soldiers line up for a charge during a reenactment of the bloody 1864 Battle of Franklin, known as the Gettysburg of the West.

His use of light reminds me of a painter using colors on a canvas, only Bob uses it to accentuate the color and texture of an image he wants to preserve and portray. In Bob's words, "One of my favorite things to do is to drive until I get lost and have to work to find my way back. That is when I have found some of my best images. While I love my work as a commercial photographer, I feel very different when I am working on my own. I love to chase the light and feel the freedom to take the pictures that touch my heart."

There are many layers to Bob's work. I appreciate the fact that Bob has a deep and abiding interest in making sure that Tennesseans understand their connection to their past. His photographs of historic buildings in our cities as well as rural sites, such as Davy Crockett's cabin, are symbols of our architectural heritage that are precious and unique to Tennessee. Bob believes deeply that we need to preserve our heritage, whether it is natural or manmade.

There used to be a sign at the Tennessee/Virginia border that read, "Welcome to the three states of Tennessee." Indeed, Tennessee is divided by the stroke of geography into three distinct areas: the Great Smoky Mountains of the East (and the part of the state that stayed with the Union during the Civil War); the plateaus and rolling hills of middle Tennessee; and the flat farmland of the Delta west to Memphis, on the banks of the Mississippi River. Bob has succeeded in capturing the distinctive characteristics of each grand area, while integrating them into a worthy portrait of our great state at the dawn of the twenty-first century.

A boot store along the Broadway Historic District in Nashville, created in 1980. Area bars and hotels were hangouts for country music performers from the 1940s to the 1970s.

LEFT: A lone boater cruises Center Hill Lake, that is surrounded by fall color. The 64-mile-long reservoir was created in 1946 when the Army Corps of Engineers dammed the Caney Fork River in Buffalo Valley.

BELOW: The Victorian tower of Anderson Hall at Maryville College, located in the Maryville, just south of Knoxville. Founded in 1819, the liberal arts college is the twelfth oldest college in the South.

RIGHT: Bass fisherman silhouetted in the early dawn on the shore of Percy Priest Lake. Named for former Tennessee congressman J. Percy Priest, the dam was dedicated by President Lyndon B. Johnson in 1968. Just fifteen minutes from downtown Nashville, the lake is a favorite local hangout.

FAR RIGHT: One of the many barns around Shelbyville, home to the world-famous Tennessee Walking Horse. Each August, the National Walking Horse Celebration is held here.

LEFT: Since Elvis Presley's death in 1977, his many fans have written out tributes on the stone wall surrounding Graceland, the 14-acre estate that was Elvis's home in Memphis. The home and grounds have been open for tours since 1982.

RIGHT: A bronze statue of Elvis is located downtown on Beale Street, where he was influenced by the area's rhythm and blues musicians. This small Elvis Park is located near Sun Records, the recording studio that made him famous.

BELOW: Elvis rests alongside other members of his family in the Meditation Garden, adjacent to the mansion. People leave flowers and stuffed animals at the gravesite daily. Each year on the eve of Elvis's death, there is a mass pilgrimage to his grave that includes a candle-lit procession through the garden.

RIGHT: Located on the west bank of the Tennessee River, the 4,000-acre Shiloh National Military Park is the site of the bloodiest battle of the Civil War. Nearly 24,000 soldiers were killed during the two-day battle in April 1862. The park also contains well-preserved Indian mounds and an extensive archaeological site.

BELOW: Mansker's Station Historic Site, a living history site in Goodlettsville, is a reconstruction of the 1779 frontier fort at one-third of its size. The site includes the original Bowen House, the oldest standing brick structure in middle-Tennessee.

LEFT: Hay rolls are silhouetted by a misty morning sunrise at Leiper's Fork. Just off the Natchez Trace Parkway, south of Nashville, Leiper's Fork is a popular stop for bicyclists and motorcyclists.

BELOW: The country between Lynnville and Cornersville is fox-hunting territory. During any given day during the fox-hunting season in winter, you will find the Hillsboro Hounds on the job. Hunt master Henry Hooker runs the hounds along a ridge to the barn, after a long day of hunting.

RIGHT: Since 1941, the Iroquois Steeplechase has been held at Percy Warner Park on the second Saturday in May. This annual celebration attracts huge crowds to watch the seven races. The race is named for the famous race horse that in 1881 was the first American horse to win the English Derby.

BELOW: The Tennessee Secondary Schools Athletic Association sponsors a Spring Fling in Chattanooga that is an annual state championship for high school spring sports. Soccer players from Ridgeway High School and Donelson Christian Academy battle for the ball during the class A-AA state soccer finals.

LEFT: Cades Cove was first settled around 1819. New settlers, drawn to the area's limestone-based soil, continued to arrive and by 1850 the population reached 700. Built in 1856, the Dan Lawson Place was surrounded by a number of outbuildings including the smokehouse pictured here.

BELOW: Wildflowers bloom abundantly in the late spring throughout the Cumberland Plateau, including these daisies and wild bitterweed. This field is found near Armathwaite, a small community just south of the Big South Fork National Recreational Area.

RIGHT: In the mid-1800s, cotton merchants built grand Victorian mansions along Adams Street near downtown Memphis. The Memphis City Beautiful Commission is housed in this mansion that was built in 1847 by Benjamin A. Massey, an early Memphis lawyer. Three other homes in the "Victorian Village" have been renovated and are now museums.

BELOW: The Agricenter International, a 1,000-acre showcase for modern agricultural technology is on the grounds of the former Shelby County Penal Farm in Memphis. These sunflowers, as well as thousands of other vegetable and flower varieties, are grown there.

ABOVE: The *General Jackson* showboat was named after the first steamboat to operate on the Cumberland River. Launched in 1985, this 300-foot paddlewheeler is remniscent of the paddlewheel steamboats that cruised the southern waterways in the 1800s. Its Victorian Theater seats 600 people for live performances and meals.

RIGHT: Behind the World's Fair, Water Park rises the 266-foot Sunsphere that was the icon of the 1982 World's Fair in Knoxville. The surrounding park is home to many shops and restaurants.

The newest addition to the Nashville skyline is BellSouth's double-spired building (on the right), affectionately referred to as the "bat building."

STOUFFER HOTEL

LEFT: Federal Express's Information Technology Campus is located in Collierville. Founded in 1971, Federal Express revolutionized the air cargo and overnight shipping business. They were the first American business to make a revenue of $1 billion within ten years.

BELOW: While there are several different colors among the Iris (Iridaceae), the purple bearded Iris was designated as the Tennessee state flower in 1933.

RIGHT: The Country Music Hall of Fame and Museum in Nashville opened in 1967, but moved to a new home in May 2001. The Hall of Fame features exhibits of country music costumes, memorabilia, and instruments and holds an extensive archive of country and folk music recorded on everything from wax cylinders to CDs. The Hall of Fame is just a few steps from 1892 Ryman Auditorium, which is known to some as the mother church of country music.

BELOW: Pigeon Forge, featuring entertainment, rides, museums, and the Dollywood theme park, has become the state's top entertainment attraction. The multi-million-dollar Country Music Tonite Theater is a 1500-seat facility that features a professional musical revue of musical styles ranging from country to gospel.

LEFT: The Cumberland Plateau cuts a 50-mile-wide swath across the state midway between Nashville and Knoxville. The area is rural, dotted with riding trails, four state parks, and a number of small to mid-sized farms.

RIGHT: All around Leiper's Fork in Williamson County on the Natchez Trace Parkway, you will find a large number of quarter horse trainers and breeders. Many championship hunters and jumpers have come from this area, including Olympic gold-medalists.

BELOW: From a mountaintop retreat in Pigeon Forge, a couple watches the sunset bathe the Great Smoky Mountains in gold.

RIGHT: The 520,408-acre Great Smoky Mountains National Park in eastern Tennessee is the most visited park in the nation, with more than two million visitors annually. When the trees turn in the fall, color sweeps from the valley floor to the mountaintops. Visitors flock to Cades Cove, and there can be bumper-to-bumper traffic on the 11-mile Cades Cove loop.

BELOW: Playing in a pile of fall leaves in Centennial Park in Nashville, an older brother makes his sister laugh. Because elevations in Tennessee vary from sea level to 6,643 feet, fall colors can be enjoyed from mid-October until late November.

LEFT: Every Christmas, more than two million lights adorn the trees and exterior of the Opryland Hotel, and storytellers and musicians perform in the interior atriums and conservatories. Visiting the hotel is a favorite holiday tradition for Nashvillians and visitors alike.

RIGHT: As fall colors fade, the bleak winter landscape of the foothills of the Great Smoky Mountains is studded with electric lights. From early November through February, Winterfest light displays, such as this one in Patriot Park, dot Pigeon Forge and Sevier County.

BELOW: The entrance of Dollywood in Pigeon Forge is lit up with this colorful butterfly, Dolly Parton's logo, during Winterfest and the Festival of Lights.

ABOVE: Go Forth Creek is one of many streams that feed into the Ocoee River. Located in southeastern Tennessee, the creek winds through the Cherokee National Forest.

RIGHT: The two-mile hike to the Chimney Tops is a short but steep 1,700-foot climb. Known to the Cherokee as the "forked antlers," the 4,755-foot Chimney Top has two spires (the two bumps silhouetted by clouds) and provides a breathtaking 360-degree view of Great Smoky Mountains National Park.

LEFT: Located in Chucalissa, this hut is located in a reconstructed American Indian village that portrays life in the area from A.D. 1000 to 1500. Here a shaman is performing a curing ceremony, while an herb potion simmers over a fire. Run by the Department of Anthropology at the University of Memphis, Chucalissa is a 187-acre national historic landmark that also houses the C. H. Nash Archaeology Museum and research facility.

BELOW: Rudy, a screech owl, is perched on a limb after a Wilderness Week workshop on raptors in Pigeon Forge. His home is the Bays Mountain Park in Kingsport, a raptor center that houses birds of prey injured in the wild. The screech owl is very small and soft, but its call is ear-piercing.

RIGHT: Formed by an earthquake in 1811, the 25,000-acre Reelfoot Lake in Tennessee's northwestern corner was previously a cypress forest, and trees can still be found above and below the water's surface. Located in the Mississippi Flyway, the lake attracts a wide variety of waterfowl, including shore and wading birds as well as golden and bald eagles.

BELOW: In late spring, fiddlehead ferns pop up all across the state. Named for the shape of the newly emerging fronds, fiddlehead ferns are commonly known as "wild ferns."

LEFT: Marie's Daylily Farm is due south of Greenville, at the foot of the Appalachian Mountains. More than 6,000 varieties of lilies are spread across the farm's rolling terrain, many of which were cultivated by Marie and her husband.

BELOW: During Fall Fest, displays constructed out of hay, corn stalks, pumpkins, and flowers are spread around Pigeon Forge.

LEFT: The three-petalled trillium is a herald of early spring in Great Smoky Mountains National Park. Older trilliums flower pink, while all the newer plants are white.

RIGHT: The Tennessee state motto is "Agriculture and Commerce." This is most evident in west Tennessee, where the flat topography supports large fields of soybeans and cotton. Soybeans are the state's top cash crop.

BELOW: Wild azaleas dot the Great Smoky Mountains with soft pink color in the early spring.

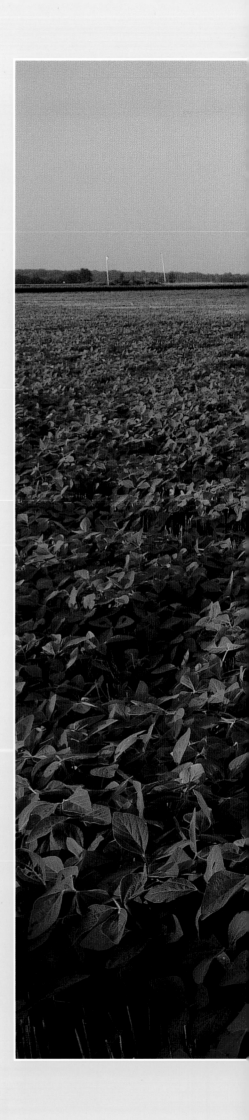

RIGHT: West of Chattanooga, Interstate 24 crosses the mist-covered Nickajack Lake. Built in 1967, the Nickajack Lake extends 46 miles up the Tennessee River and is part of the stairstep system of reservoirs and locks on the river designed to facilitate barge travel.

BELOW: Every summer weekend, thousands of whitewater enthusiasts flock to the Hiawassee River, near Reliance, to kayak, canoe, raft, or just tube. With only class I and II rapids, the river is a great place for beginning whitewater paddlers.

RIGHT: The Old Mill, which still grinds thousands of pounds of grains daily, is a popular stop in Pigeon Forge. Built on the bank of the Little Pigeon River in 1830, the mill produced meal and flour and even supplied electricity for Pigeon Forge until 1935.

BELOW: Only 6,059 white oak barrels fit into the barrel houses at the Jack Daniel's Distillery in Lynchburg. The Distillery, the oldest in the country, was registered in 1866. Wooden barrels give the whiskey its amber color and mellow flavor.

LEFT: A light snow blankets the harvested fields just outside of Clarksville. Snow in middle-Tennessee is rare, which makes it a memorable experience for children.

BELOW: The 200-year-old downtown is one Franklin's main attractions. The downtown is anchored by this 1926 Franklin Post Office, which has recently become home to the William County Arts Council and the Heritage Foundation of Franklin.

RIGHT: This 360-degree view of the Great Smoky Mountains is payoff for the rugged 2½-mile hike to Andrew's Bald. The scene pictured is just part of the view from the 4,746-foot summit.

BELOW: This statue, located in Morningside Park in Knoxville, commemorates biographer, scriptwriter, and author Alex Haley, who grew up in Tennessee. Haley gained national fame after his novel *Roots* was published in 1976 and was made into a television miniseries in 1977.

ABOVE: Over millions of years, the Ocoee River has cut a steep, winding channel into this rocky mountainside, which you can see when the Tennessee Valley Authority diverts water from the river to produce hydroelectric power. On weekends, thousands flock to the Ocoee Whitewater Center, where the 1996 Olympic canoe and kayak competition was held.

RIGHT: Cravath Hall is in the center of the Fisk University campus. Built in 1929 as a library, the building was recently renovated and now houses the campus administration. Founded in 1867, Fisk University is the home of the Fisk Jubilee Singers.

ABOVE: Ayers Hall has become the symbol for the University of Tennessee in Knoxville. Named for former university president, Brown Ayers, the building was erected in 1921 on the highest point on campus.

RIGHT: Along the state's western border, towboats push barges up and down the Mississippi River 24 hours a day. Here, the bluffs of Memphis are silhouetted in the sunset.

BELOW: A pair of ducks have an early morning swim in Willow Pond in the 2,685-acre Percy Warner Park.

LEFT: Morton Overlook on the Newfound Gap Road oversees the misty Sugerlands Valley below. The road, a WPA project in 1930, divides Great Smoky Mountains National Park in two.

BELOW: Meet Ya Ya, one of two giant pandas that came from China to visit the Memphis Zoo. James Sasser, former U.S. senator and ambassador to China, helped arrange the visit.

RIGHT: Beale Street in Memphis has been home to the blues for nearly a century. Soon after W. C. Handy wrote the first blues song in 1909, blues bands filled the clubs. Famous blues performers followed, including Bobby "Blue" Bland, Alberta Hunter, Albert King, Muddy Waters, and the "King of the Blues" B. B. King. Today you can also hear newer sounds, including fusion jazz and reggae.

BELOW: The Chattanooga Choo Choo engine on display at Chattanooga Terminal Station is the same wood-burning locomotive used on the first run from Cincinnati to Chattanooga in 1880. Saved from the wrecking ball in 1973, the terminal has become a unique vacation destination where you can dine and sleep in authentic rail cars.

LEFT: Carnton Mansion is behind the 1,481 marked graves of Confederate soldiers wounded in the Battle of Franklin. Before the Civil War, the mansion was host to many dignitaries, including Andrew Jackson and Sam Houston. After the Battle of Franklin, local homeowner Caroline McGavok rolled up the carpets to house more than 200 wounded soldiers.

BELOW: Farmlands dot Rutherford County, southeast of Nashville. These fertile farmlands, however, are being replaced in recent years by buildings and roads as corporate offices and manufacturing facilities are moving here.

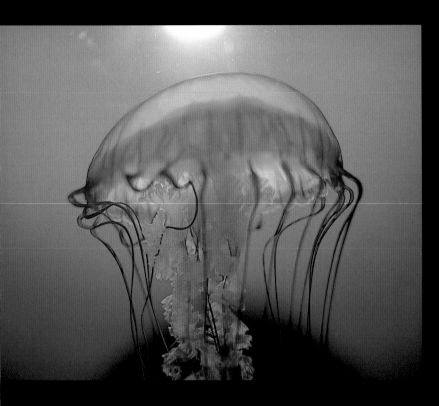

ABOVE: What is a jellyfish doing in landlocked
Tennessee? It is part of an exhibit on the varieties of jellyfish at the Tennessee Aquarium
in Chattanooga. More than 9,000 animals
populate this 400,000-gallon aquarium.

RIGHT: The Thomas Divide, a long ridge
along the Newfound Gap Road, overlooks
the Ocolonee Valley.

LEFT: This wind-twisted cedar tree hangs over the Cumberland River. This bluff, which rises above the Ashland City Highway, overlooks farms along River Road.

BELOW: Falls Hollow is aptly named. From the main waterfall, numerous streams run downhill, flow off the slate ledge, and merge into one larger stream.

RIGHT: The Memphis dream home of Piggly Wiggly founder Clarence Saunders is called the Pink Palace because it is made of pink Georgian marble. When the unfinished building was given to the city in the late 1920s, the palace became home to a decorative arts museum.

BELOW: Leaving his tailor shop in Greenville for a life in politics, Andrew Johnson was Abraham Lincoln's vice president in 1865 and was thrown into the presidency when Lincoln was assassinated. The so-called "Radical Republicans" opposed his plans for reconstructing the South after the Civil War and tried to impeach him in 1868. He was acquitted by one vote.

ABOVE: Morning sun tops the Union Planters building in the Memphis skyline and lights the mist hovering over the Mississippi River. Best viewed from Arkansas, the Memphis skyline is silhouetted against the orange sky.

ABOVE: From the bluff district overlooking the Tennessee River, you can see rowing teams from the University of Tennessee at Chattanooga practice nearly every morning.

RIGHT: Tod Carter went to war for the Confederates. During the Battle of Franklin, Carter's family huddled in the basement of their home while the battle raged all around the house. When the smoke cleared, Carter was found wounded, only 200 feet from this back door. He died two days later.

BELOW: Hibiscus grows wild in the shallow waters of Reelfoot Lake. An important national wildlife refuge, the lake has the largest concentration of wintering bald eagles in the U.S.

LEFT: An old canoe sits on the bank of the pond on Montpellier Farm near Franklin.

BELOW: At one of the many quarter horse farms near Leiper's Fork, two young colts frolic with their mothers.

LEFT: To brighten the winter, Nashville celebrates the Antique and Garden Show, a fundraiser for Cheekwood Botanical Gardens. Daniel Ost, a floral artist from Belgium, was brought in for the show and an exhibit at Cheekwood.

BELOW: May is the month to find the large, white blooms of magnolias. Magnolia are so fragrant that just one bloom will fill a house with its sweet scent.

ABOVE: Tobacco hanging in a barn to dry is a sure sign of fall, although pink morning glories
indicate that the weather has not yet turned cold. Smithville, in the heart of the Cumberland
Plateau, feels the temperature changes in early fall, ahead of the rest of the state.

LEFT: Sun rises over the Foothills Parkway. The parkway runs along a ridge in the Appalachian foothills, just outside Great Smoky Mountains National Park.

BELOW: Center Hill Lake has maintained its pristine appearance because the Army Corps of Engineers banned dock-building and the cutting of trees on the lake's edge and mandated that buildings must be set back from the shoreline.

BELOW: Davy Crockett was born August 17, 1786, east of Greeneville on the banks of the Nolichucky River, near the mouth of Limestone Creek. This site features a re-creation of his cabin and a museum built by the Tennessee State Parks.

ABOVE: During the French and Indian War from 1754 to 1763, Fort Loudoun was constructed in order to persuade the Overhill Cherokee Nation to fight against the French. In August 1760, when relations broke down between South Carolina and the Cherokees, the fort fell to the Cherokees. This frontier fort has been reconstructed on the shores of Tellico Lake near Vonore.

ABOVE: Collector George Gruhn has a comprehensive collection of vintage guitars. His business, Gruhn Guitars, has a client list that includes celebrities such as Johnny Cash, Eric Clapton, Vince Gill, George Harrison, Paul McCartney, and Neil Young. "There is a greater depth of appreciation with musical instruments than with almost any other collectable," says Gruhn. "A guitar responds to the individual player and sounds completely different when you play it than when you listen to someone else play it."

BELOW: Wooden baskets hold the fall harvest of apples at the Farmers' Market in Nashville. Now located at the Bicentennial Mall, the market has broadened its selections to include various ethnic foods.

RIGHT: Jackson Falls is a natural waterslide as it cascades down these smooth rocks. As you walk down into this hollow from the Natchez Trace Parkway, the air temperature drops thanks to the cold waters of Jackson Branch. It is named for Andrew Jackson because it was his favorite stop along the Natchez Trace.

BELOW: The Ocoee Whitewater Center, with its natural and artificial rapids, has become a premier whitewater venue for athletes from all over the world. The canoe and kayaking competitions of the 1996 Summer Olympics were held here.

LEFT: Bears, deer, owls, wild turkeys and many other animals can be found along the 110-mile loop of Cades Cove. From early morning until 10 A.M. on Wednesdays and Saturdays, the viewing is better as bicycles are the only vehicles allowed in the cove.

BELOW: A strip of land between Kentucky Lake and Lake Barkley was converted by the Tennessee Valley Authority into a long vertical park that stretches north from Paris, Tennessee, up to Grand Rivers, Kentucky. Land Between the Lakes offers boating, camping, fishing, and mountain biking.

RIGHT: The Lynchburg Hardware & General Store is located on the square, across from the Moore County courthouse. The store, which proclaims that it is where "all goods worth price charged," still has a Coke for a dime. One of the many barrel houses of the Jack Daniels Distillery stands on the hill above the store.

BELOW: Tennessee weather can change overnight. February can be so warm that trees and flowers begin blooming, then the next day, it will snow.

LEFT: Lake Watauga is in the middle of Centennial Park in Nashville. A favorite lunchtime picnicking or jogging spot, the park was the site of the Tennessee centennial celebration in 1896.

BELOW: Young ballet dancers pose by one of the three large ponds at the Botanical Gardens at Cheekwood. The original Cheekwood gardens were designed by local landscape architect Bryant Fleming. Recently redesigned, the ponds were renamed the Robinson Family Water Garden and feature hardy water plants, lotuses, and shade-loving perennials.

RIGHT: Jonesborough had been established for seventeen years before Tennessee became the sixteenth state in 1796, making it the oldest town in the state. The citizens of Jonesborough, which was originally the county seat of Washington County, thought they were not being fairly represented so they formed their own state called the State of Franklin, which became part of Tennessee. Much of Jonesborough has been preserved and is now filled with antique shops and bed-and-breakfast inns.

BELOW: When Andrew Johnson left the White House, the nation's seventeenth president moved to this house in Greenville, just a few blocks from his first home and tailor shop. The house is now open to the public as part of the Andrew Johnson Historic Site.

ABOVE: In 1938, the Farm Security Administration acquired 1,720 acres to provide a recreational area for the families around Crossville, which became Cumberland Mountain State Park. Built by the Conservation Corps, this dam was constructed to form Byrd Lake.

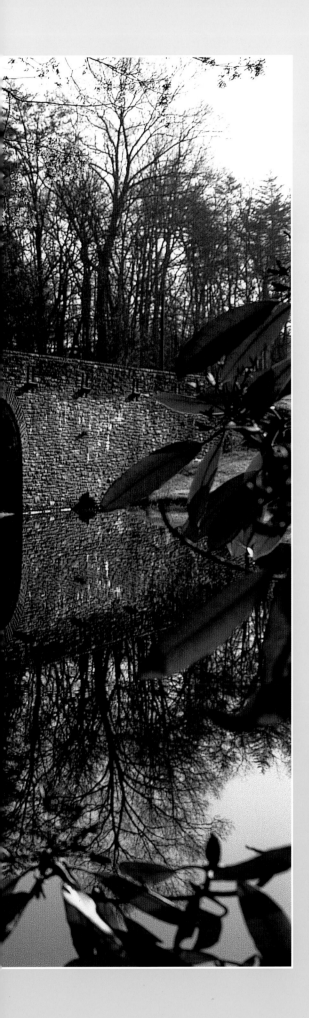

ABOVE: Roan Mountain straddles the line between Tennessee and North Carolina. Part of the Appalachian Trail runs through the three mountaintops in Roan Mountain State Park: Grassy Bald, Jane Bald, and Round Bald. A hiker and his dog climb the log steps to the top of Round Bald.

RIGHT: In 1541, Hernando de Soto is said to have had his first glimpse of the Mississippi River from here. Thanks to the river transportation, trains, and now air freight, Memphis is known as "America's Distribution Center."

BELOW: These statues in front of the Shelby County Courthouse may look familiar–they have appeared in many John Grisham movies that were shot in Memphis.

LEFT: Huddling around the fire for warmth, these actors have braved a 20-degree morning to help recreate the Battle of Franklin.

BELOW: Misty mornings are magic in the Great Smoky Mountains. This shot is from Newfound Gap Road, the 33-mile route that traverses Great Smoky Mountains National Park. Newfound Gap separates Tennessee from North Carolina.

LEFT: On the evening of April 4, 1968, in Memphis, American history was altered forever. On the balcony of the Lorraine Motel, Dr. Martin Luther King Jr. had stepped out of his room for dinner when a shot rang out. In 1991, the Lorraine Motel became a part of the National Civil Rights Museum.

RIGHT: Nissan's first U.S. manufacturing facility was built in Smyrna. Since it's opening in 1980, the Smyrna plant has grown to 5.4 million square feet and assembles five different models.

BELOW: A regulation basketball is covered with 96,000 nubs—the same number that covers this ball hanging over the 1999 Women's Basketball Hall of Fame in Knoxville.

LEFT: Once a day, the hand-carved Clyde Park Miniature Circus comes to life in the Pink Palace Museum, thanks to hundreds of hidden ropes and pulleys.

BELOW: As the hot, steamy summer yields to the cool fall, the deciduous trees color the state with brilliant yellows, reds, and oranges.

RIGHT: Civil War cannons overlook the Tennessee River and downtown Chattanooga in Point Park, located at the top of Lookout Mountain. Here, on November 24, 1863, a layer of fog descended into the Tennessee River Valley just before the strategic "Battle Above the Clouds" erupted, allowing the Confederates to defend the mountain against the Union troops.

BELOW: Silhouetted against the evening sky, this statue in Legislative Plaza commemorates the strength and determination of Tennessee's women during the "War Between the States." Sculpted by Belle Kinney, the statue celebrates the women who helped nurse, clothe, and feed soldiers, while running farms and businesses.

LEFT: This tobacco farm at mile 401 on the Natchez Trace Parkway features this exhibit on tobacco growing. In the fall, the plants are hung in this old barn to dry.

BELOW: Ducktown, in the southeast corner of the state, became a virtual moonscape in the heyday of copper smelting when 100 tons a day of copper ore was smelted here in cauldrens like this one. Today hundreds of acres of foliage have been reclaimed and the Burra Burra Copper Mine, which operated from 1899 to 1959, is a historical industrial site.

RIGHT: Every Friday and Saturday night, the longest-running live radio show goes on the air from stage of the 4,400-seat Grand Ole Opry House. Each winter, the show that originated in Nashville in 1925 is broadcast from the renovated 1892 Ryman Auditorium, its home from 1943 to 1974 before it moved to the opera house.

BELOW: Designed to resemble the monument of Lysicrates in Athens, Greece, the tower of the 1859 Tennessee State Capitol is a distinctive landmark in the Nashville skyline.

LEFT: In June 1954, the Old Hickory Dam was completed and the lake began to fill. The dam consists of a powerhouse (left), spillway, and navigation lock. The dam is located on the Cumberland River, 25 miles from downtown Nashville.

BELOW: Barges head into Old Hickory Lake, after exiting the lock that raises the water level 60 feet from the Cumberland River.

RIGHT: When water from the Ocoee River is diverted for power, it reveals a dramatic riverbed of golden limestone. Thousands of years of water in the gorge have worn smooth the layers and folds of rock.

BELOW: A young boy cools off in the lower waterfall at Fall Hollow, mile 392 on the Natchez Trace Parkway.

LEFT: A rare Porter 2-4-2 locomotive is displayed at the renovated Cowan Depot train museum at the base of Monteagle Mountain in the Cumberland Mountains. A helper locomotive was attached at the depot to get the train over the mountain toward Chattanooga.

BELOW: The Hunter Museum of American Art sits high on a bluff over the Tennessee River. The sculpture garden features a collection of twentieth-century sculpture.

RIGHT: Southern yellow wood sorrel spreads across the field of a Williamson County Farm.

BELOW: From the upper falls, the water of Jackson Falls flows across a ledge and plunges into a deep pool below.

In this view
from the
Cumberland
Plateau,
Rockwood is
shrouded in
fog, and in
the distance
you can see
the foothills
of the Great
Smoky
Mountains.